Firebird Baltic Blue

Helga Jermy
Firebird Baltic Blue

Acknowledgements

The following poems from this collection have previously been
published and my thanks are extended to the editors,
Nathan Hondros, Lucy Dougan and Martin Langford:
'Second Skin' previously published in *Regime Magazine of New
Writing*, Regime Books, Western Australia
'Saaremaa' previously published in the *Australian Poetry
Member's Anthology 2014*

'Baltic Fox' was longlisted for the UK National Poetry Prize 2016.

Special thanks are extended to Kristen Lang for many helpful
suggestions when discussing the final edit of this collection.

This collection is dedicated to Pete and Sophie Jermy
for their ongoing love and support.

Firebird Baltic Blue
ISBN 978 1 76041 476 4
Copyright © text Helga Jermy 2017
Cover design: Helga Jermy

First published 2017 by
GINNINDERRA PRESS
PO Box 3461 Port Adelaide 5015 Australia
www.ginninderrapress.com.au

Contents

Introduction	7
Baltic Blue	9
The Idea of Lingonberry	11
Fable	13
Second Skin	14
Another reality	15
Diversion	16
Terviseks	18
Life and its antonym	19
Saaremaa	20
Far North	21
Tallinn	22
The Road to Parnu	24
Dew and Salt	25
One Two Three	26
The day we feasted with grandmother	27
Philosophy of the Hare	28
Kadriorg Park	29
Reflecting	30
Lupine Light	31
Spruce	32
Mourning Song	34
Edge of the ice	35
Legless on the Toompea Hill	36
Toompea	37
Lingonberry	38
Old Town Squared and Cobbled	39
Twilight	40
Suspended	41
Laneway at Night	42

Moon in the first quarter	43
Everything Changes	44
Adrift	46
Exclusions	47
Flights swarming	48
Fake Moon, Red Foxed	49
Firebird	**51**
First Impressions Through a Kaleidoscope	55
Maps	57
Sunset Behind St Olaf's With Chemicals	59
Night Poetry	60
We could have been harlequins	61
The Sea	62
Baltic Fox	63
The glorious white of light	65

Introduction

Denied access to a place, by necessity you invent it.

Visiting my father's country, Estonia, after his death was a kind of haunting and a constant juggle of focus between the blurred stories and a new reality which can never truly be my reality but, regardless, shapes and completes a sense of identity and belonging.

These poems emerge from family history, brief excursions, flexible truths, myth and secret longings. The final section includes poems that evolve from tangential thoughts and fabulations inspired by Estonian poetry, especially the early twentieth-century theories and innovations of the Siuru (Firebird) group.

These are the stories and the imaginings of a crossing into a new but strangely familiar territory, and a tribute to my dad, Mihkel Talts, and all my extended Baltic family.

Baltic Blue

I want to press my face to the
cracked pane of my home window.
– Kalju Lepik

The Idea of Lingonberry

If I want to taste
the idea of lingonberry
it is for its location
in Saaremaa and sparse
Finnish pine forests
where its plump red
syllables
bleed into earth.

I took you there once
on a plane in a dream
the long way round
so we could travel south

to where the elk and lynx
navigate fables.
We didn't see them
though still we believe,
hear footprints
stepping through
syntax and needle frost
into fresh narrative.

If I catch a plane there
I depend on cartographers
on sleek engineering
on civil exchanges of currency
on presumptions
of policy and the modern plague
of governments.

We could just let the Swedes
make a jam of it
squeeze its juice into profit
ship it into containers
with soft slices of wood
and unfathomable instructions.

Fable

The letters arrived via Soviet post,
Rapla Rajoon postmark
and smelling of chemical ink.
Russian stamps on Eesti lines
held in a curious glue.
Sometimes books would arrive too;
first fairy tales, then pictorials
that smiled with factory girls who obviously
loved their work.
Dad told me to look for signs between
the lines, him being no fan of propaganda. But
the folklore took him elsewhere,
somewhere where the world was less wary,
the trees a pine-pricked memory,
the beasts so clearly friend or foe.

      To dear me from dear cousins: 'the
lakes are frozen, we skied to school today, it
is the birthday of a faraway aunt, we're
waiting for the ice to thaw.'
One day, I told myself, one day…
until one day a fox, a lynx and a wolf walked me
into a Thomas Cook, then left me to it.

Second Skin

The Baltics, 1981

I felt that slip before　as we were herded
into the cattle barn departure lounge of
St Petersburg　then Leningrad　and they
said you looked like Pushkin and took you
off for questioning　a search through
souvenirs　and I felt the icy fear of the gulags
fury for the lost ten years of my *vanavanemad*
held captive in the desolate bear hug of Siberia
and you returned and slipped me back　laughed
at the quaintness of their paranoia　drank
tea from their samovars　I smiled behind a
mask as they stamped and displayed their armoury.

I slipped before as a tear let show the squeaky
shed skin of *Taat*'s *isamaa*　new cultural cloak
a flimsy guise　pinned, scarred, grieved.
I zip my skin　this thorny raw hide　this gabardine
against cold war and distant rain　until my skin
begins to itch again or the hungry growl of
the bear creeps back into my dreams.

vanavanemad – grandparents
Taat – father
isamaa – homeland

Another reality

Tallinn 2014
for Piret

I watch you in cobbled streets
striding ahead through
a life which could be mine,

you, who are such an expert in the language
I could have spoken,
pointing out the missing landmarks

and the best view of the port.
Medieval walls and red turrets
hold negative spaces of light.

We're heading for a pasta lunch,
pork blood and barley porridge
stored away in a bowl of culinary myth.

My stomach grumbles.
Your smile is familial.
We both love the smell of lilies.

Somewhere south of here on a quiet farm
our futures were squashed between titans of war.
Like insect wings, brief histories glow in amber.

Diversion

It is a slow drive
without answers.
The taxi driver
doesn't speak English.
Why should he?
19? 20?

He would rather be anywhere
than here
weaving a channel
through rush hour traffic
fiddling with a GPS.

We're no help at all.
Mute on the back seat.

His fingers tap
on a steering wheel.

At the corner
a group of headscarved women
stride their determination
towards the bakery.

What is their story
these women who have lost men
to battle lines,
lost years in spin and crookery,
eyes lowered?

Daughters held their silence
in wool and cotton,
song festivals
beat their impatience
into coroneted memory skirts.

A huddle of men
kick the barriers,
curse the blockades.

A president will visit soon.

The sun glares at it all.
Heat is a mystery here.
Barricades are not.
This morning in another time
reinvents the blurred edges.

A hotel emerges in a sweaty haze.
In a fuddle we figure out the euros.

Terviseks

Our hosts are generous. Unfamiliar cousins
with names from myths and fairy tales.
Our plane lands at four, by five we are collected,
marched and feted like VIP tourists,
by nine our worries about eating
pickled herrings and blood pancakes
turn to disappointment
when they are not on the menu.
We perch on battlements
clink our glasses with a new word –
Terviseks! – drink Tallinn liqueur,
look down on a view to die for.
Many did, of course.
Switchblade of war slicing through families,
pushing the tides of migration,
staining the landscape red.
So strange to walk these cobbled streets.
So strange to see my face
reflected in the faces of strangers,
to hold the hands of aunts
who held the hand of my father.

Terviseks – cheers

Life and its antonym

They killed the bears. We are shocked.
Not for food, not to cull. Just because.

Their seats are nicely rugged now. Soft furry
warmth against penetrating cold. We don't understand.

A stuffed head has glass eyes that seem to carry a soul,
a parody of life laid out on a table.

There is tourist potential. American shooters
lured by the deep woods, the lack of laws.

Back home, bear claws, wolf skin, the flesh
of wild boars begin to stalk me. I ate the boar.

Pared back like a sore; a taste, a thrill, a thirst.
The bear mouth with its fish. A thorn in my fur.

Saaremaa

I steal your stories
but it is a reverent kind of theft.
It feels like inheritance after loss,
greeted by trees that walk
in fables, Saaremaa gods born
from falling meteorites,
all those tales washed in from the sea.
I look only for geography as we drive
through the heart of this land,
but each tree holds a clue in its DNA.
I welcome the fading light
as it stops painting shadows.
I can reach for the dark here.
It is a warm dark, sepia, its fear
and possibilities calmed somehow.

Far North

The north wind suits you.
Salt mist peppers your dreams,
sea water runs through your veins
with herring and eel.
From your coat snow crystals float
like the falling down
of flying geese,
drifts over frozen lakes
to melt on pelts of elk.
For you the northern lights
above your dawn,
crisp snow beneath
your morning footprints.

Tallinn

The sky unfolds its moods on us, tumbling black into blue,
then crisp and sharp as a paper crane.
Today, military planes shoot through wisps of frayed cotton
shaking the cornflower blue.
The air gasps here. A throaty grumble.
I'm looking for spies while the locals just buy flowers.
In myths the forests walk away here, move shards
of timber needles in a lumbering dance
to where the earth is friendlier.
Trees stand to attention as you pass by.
You believe their intention. Christmas trees with eyes.
Bears and wild boar are fair game for hunters.
The name for wolf is hunt.
Lynx eyes watch from spruce limbs,
feline grace draped in a trapper's prize,
ears streaked black and pulled to a quizzical point,
sickle claws hide in soft mittens.
Dreams are hard-won here. Look east, look west,
Tallinn's red roofs and turrets stand fast
within their ancient walls.
Dense walls have been left here,
gardens, turrets and gilded armoury
too anchored to this land to flee their history.
Relics jar with glassed-over bomb disfigurement.
Sound shell echoes with cotton skirts,
the herringbone unruffled.
I catch my heel on a slab of concrete revivalism.
Tomorrow Obama will visit.

Schoolboys practise their drill and smiles,
cute as naval buttons. Presidential faces
make improbable babushkas.
The flag flies white, black and blue; not bruised
but a blanket of snow, trees and sky.

The Road to Parnu

Signposts flash by in a foreign language.
An old lady disembarks after
words with the driver. I am clueless.
Inside the coach the Rs roll in absence of hills
stress is on the first syllable,
rhythm is strangely familiar.
I catch the lyricism and it is enough,
a chiding reminder that with a little effort on my part
those rhymes and patterns would talk to me too.
But I am deaf to meaning,
only the spoken music to pass away the hours.

Dew and Salt

Wood piles in a rural shed
with dreams of splintering the backside of winter.
Its hollows crawl with rodent surplus.
There are eyes in the long log
soulful as boxed Lepidoptera.
Perhaps the dogs will chase, perhaps they won't,
a first course before the feckless hare.
Ancient lanes wave to the chopped sea.
Sloped roofs toss off a threat of snow.
Sheltered by walls and the sleepless trees
a garden stretches out its naked dreams
to a rare promise of sun.

One Two Three

Uks   kaks   kolm
We are determined to learn something
Neli   viis   kuus
(all those years I was sure it was goose).
One day we will visit the graves of the poets,
translate the hearts of Under and Lepik.

My brother wanders down the tram
to buy *neli* tickets,
is undone asking for Nellie anything,
puts 5 fingers up for 4 passes and loses it.

The locals are so far removed
from English humour,
faces polite and confused
as we spill laughter over grey smoke
under overhead sparks.

Recomposed, we disembark as directed
at the statue that overlooks
drowned souls in the bay.
Neli tourists chastened before an angel.

The day we feasted with grandmother

Thirty-three years have passed
and what I remember most
is the poem in the air; just a hint
amongst sighs and smiles,
gestures and patient translations.
Fingers entwined like vines,
we ate with just one hand,
afraid to let go as we drank
the health of the dead.
Her hands were blue-veined maps,
a transparent and delicate journey,
her solemn widow's black
defied by wild grey hair.
The day that photos came alive
she gave me crocheted slippers,
the colour of wild cranberries
picked from the frost and
hooked into cream.

Philosophy of the Hare

it is rare, the mountain hare
often mistaken for snow-melt
or a breath of wind in the grass

today it stops its race
across summer tracks to ponder
the slowness of us

he is gone in a trick of light
an outpouring of sun a conjuror's cloak
stillness spills into the space

a drum roll from a passing bus
sang to velvet ears
and we are left a flick of silver

Kadriorg Park

Another palace,
another president,
another park
named for a tsarina
another statue,
(this time a god for poetry
in the middle
of a field of day trippers).
Belvedere Apollo
with fig leaf
stone cape and laurels
defending
in a line of conifers.
This seems as good
a place as any to pull out
a tablet, to fiddle with
mood, meaning
and enjambments.
At the swan pond,
cygnets are unfamiliar
with metaphor
and sing on regardless.

Reflecting

Only in the dense light
do we become forest,
our long shadows thrown across clearings,
fingers clawing at the dirt.
We could take the easy route
on steel pathways
sleek as barn swallow dance
but choose the twisted trail
of old footprints,
follow the smell of berries
and mushrooms,
feel needles in our back,
dry earth solid under our roots.
The lines on our map
wave across like winced nerves,
branches blurring to new horizons.
I will find my own way out,
find my own way back,
and when we return to pine
the sky will still wink back
through a scratch of iris blue.

Lupine Light

It isn't hard to imagine you here amongst the pine cast
shadows, or out in the once were fields with sickle and hoe.
I saw it all in your scars; the toil and joy, metal and man, wheat

and the hungry crow, the circadian cycle of industry
and survival, lakes freezing, thawing, freezing, thawing,
the familial and the interloping fear.

The wolves have moved in to occupy your space now.
There is lupine light shining back across the hungry hills
scouring hollows for carrion, howling at the cream curdled moon.

You are safe here, warm, interiored,
far away from the ice floes and the threat of war.
Lakes are sinine soft and sacred, fish scales slicked in oil shale,

farmers displaced, hunters too fat on pork
and *viru* beer to bother you. At the edge of forest
pups play in broken saunas and old barns hold the truth of swallows.

Spruce

i

we are like fallen leaves, needlecast,
under the height of the spruce
stars are birds perched sleeping

ii

tall pines sharp as pencils
sketch charcoal spirals
contre jour against a high of light

iii

they made spruce beer for sailors
gum resin frankincense
to ward off scurvy, cheer Christmas

iv

in raw winter hoarfrost
sharpens needles
coats the silent hare

v

soundboard of pianos
timbered planed resonant
the echo of empty forests

vi

where the forest brothers
laid secrets in layers of earth
spruce roots link arms

Mourning Song

Photographs are shown to us
with great care, until she makes
air crosses over dead faces.

We descend into cathedral quiet.
She folds arms across her chest
as if to draw in a lost son,

and lets go of something vocal,
something like a hare's cry
or the sound of tyre rubber

on tarmac before the crash,
the taste of a kiss on cold flesh
in an open casket,

a visceral ache of love and regret,
a few notes escaping
into skin and bone.

It is a brief song from another life.
She pulls it back in, beats her chest
as if to tame it.

We are left with photographs.
And flowers she gave us,
each petal a lost hour on the clock.

Edge of the ice

The edge of the ice has lost its jagged skirt
sharp and clean as vitreous detachment.

We watch as it crashes into waves
drifts into a leaking kind of sleep
in the genuflecting sea, a holy ocean,
accepted like a sacrificial dream.

Feather ice still clings to needles,
a chance of accidental bloodletting.

These are ancient rituals
slippery and extreme,
a cracked world shape shifting its mood
in bergs and sheets, caps and frazil.

From here, silence rings like a bell,
lynx breath exhales in crystals.

Legless on the Toompea Hill

A kink in the road map
Short Leg or Long Leg Streets
Either way you're blistered
Climbing or meandering to turrets
Shadows running ahead, tripping on cobbles
Stony
      Steeped
              Boot polished
                      Skinned
Ahead a pink castle
Power house wrapped in rules
Red roof tiles mosaic the skyline
Chain mail shapes the fortress chairs
Clink the champagne glass of reunion
Going down again
Deflates the bubbles

Toompea

Looking down over battlements
from the walled Toompea
it seems the fairy tale can't end.
The soldiers marched in two by two
goose steps and ideologies.
Fat Margaret is named for a Danish queen,
orthodox spinnerets the work of gods and czars.
The Swedes will tell you they owned this land.
We hold blood from the iron age.
Just three days and I own the place.

We are foot sore walking
the paths of merchants and guards.
Callous and sickle scars gone soft.
The restaurant doorman does not buy
into the dream, despite the turret
above his head from which gold ringlets
should fall. We are left
to push open steel bars ourselves,
to leave by the door we came through.

Lingonberry

bitter sweet, the lingonberry
juice breaks the fibrous heart
of the dead wild boar

tenderises the stale air
adorns the forest floor
clings both to soft leaves and thorns

pink dew lingers on smiles
before the tart sap
startles in its flame-wild colours

Old Town Squared and Cobbled

Shadowy quadrant of a dream
between the dog-eared pages
      of a lithographed urban fairy tale.
Here have stood
the Teutonic, knighted,
      Dominicans, ordained,
enchanters, warlocks,
stags, identity thieves,
traders, evaders & Hanseatic legends.

Unmapped interiors hold the amber-lit
      souls of pilgrims.

Pristine butters the walls;
a fantasist's scenography,
      burgher buildings, crafty guilds,
wooden quarters of vague ownership,
skyline spired and curlicued
      into serpentine clouds.
Timelines pool in cracked stones
where a boy is busy now
      popping bubbles.

Air caught in glycerine and soap
seizes the living daylights,
      sunshine yellow.

Twilight

There is cobalt night beyond the hill,
across the flat
the blurring of sound edges

there is a shimmer of raging sun
before its wet descent,
the pooling of stars in the shadows

the streets click clack
in the twilight hollows,
we're all eclipsed in the failing lamps

but look! Abandoned tables and linen-
wrapped chairs are still
suspended in time in the marketplace

no vandal eyes erase the calm civility,
crowds disperse into cubes and attics

Suspended

*
*
*

Suspension in ice
is a magic trick
with proteins.

There is nothing to do but dream here.
Roads are severed with scratched limbs,
rivers raw and impenetrable, the sea glacial.

We are poleaxed
with beaver brains
and hare's breath.

Roads north/south are blizzard fogged,
ice cubed fish and seals just sleep.
We are unseasoned. Wind is a skewering.

Laneway at Night

A big M is blocking history
        Red against the night's medieval tower

The flower stands are shuttered
        Music an undecided rhythm

In an ancient laneway
        We are encouraged to feel leather goods

Meat arrives with pitchers of beer
        Froth spills   so do voices

Windows and doors are old
        Putty hardened like granite and gritty

Although there are no ghosts
        There is a haunting in the gallery

A curtain shivers   furniture creaks
        Birds screech across the still night

Everything is exposed
        I eat organs   feel their decay

Moon in the first quarter

Moon in the first quarter
and we are due to leave before
the unbarred light
slips into autumn.

Leaves curl and tumble resplendent
in their dying colour
like moth wings

drifting down in the sound of fall,
a scatter of stolen syllables.

Fears are voiced
about the forthcoming ice.

Tanks on the border go unspoken.

Clouds pass by, hold us briefly
in their coffin shadows,
unshroud us and travel east.

Everything Changes

In the privacy of our hotel room
all seems squared and cubed,
plumbing singing to the fridge.

We strain to see the old city skyline,
our noses pressed against the cold
glass promise of a view.

Outside traffic blurs towards
grey towers, their orange interiors
hidden like stolen fruit in winter.

Downy covers will always hide
the stripped hard metal of a bed
but we sleep as a light flickers.

In the hallway photos of stars
form a galaxy from the west,
dreams are always black and white.

Our attention wandered while
you counted the days and we
complained about the cost of flights.

We see you now heading from
London to the Lakes, freedom
all packed in a joint carry-on.

The boys are grown and shrug
at talk of politics and power.
Everything changes, they say.

They talk about cars and babies,
juggle three languages, park their
BMWs beside the new brick pizzeria

just left of barbed wire. Fences are illusions
they say. Their kids laugh and
celebrate return to school day.

Adrift

I would like to visit you
        in snowfall
hear the clean whistle
of the swimming wolf
nosing through drifts
see the weighted
branches dance   in the northern winds
watch piles of silence
        wash the landscape clean.

The world is peeled back from snow now,
a plum heart beating
              berries on the vine
tipsy as a bingeing summer.

        An elk looks me in the eye
an eye as deep as oil shale at the bottom
of Lake Peipsi
        glinting.

Exclusions

tree blood is the sap
of this land,
      rivers turning orange,
to hold life in honeycomb cells

our goodbyes hang off branches,
in the space between
      breathing and dying,
melt briefly in the hot plasma of sun

inclusions in amber require resin,
millennia,
      a certain trap in time,
an acquiescence to tears

we are exclusions, far from stillness,
pulses leap,
      take flight
across the backbone of clouds

Flights swarming

tannoy announces an open gate
obedient we're as roped goats
in our carbon guzzling
                bedazzled engine belly
grazing the light through port windows
star bored aft, stern lined and ruled

scattered the plane flies to air
black bewinged bumble flight
we're all back on
                terra zero firmer
crowds swarm, slowly traffic to grey lines
homeward edges portent

Fake Moon, Red Foxed

My tendency
to skate on illusory ice
over lakes
to the platinum woods
of fringe dwellers
revises once in a while.

Audio codecs were
conceived in these woods.
Everything interconnecting
in waves.

I could carry this too far
miss the connection
at the continental drift
fake a common moon
red fox colour a russet furphy
when all I really want to say is
none of this is real
corncrakes don't really nest in fur
claws don't quickstep into blades
don't you think
the Himalayan strawberry
has perked up this year
and,
oh,
I miss you…

Firebird

shoes made of glass –
I hear their ringing steps
coming right at me.
– Marie Under

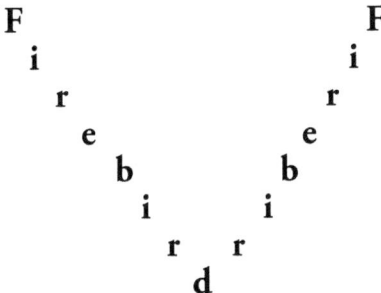

    blue feathers blazing
              on a cellar door
our love is shaped
& pebbled as street night

        worlds flush by

    clubs are hidden
in nameless alleys
Siuru!
Siuru!
the heart bursts

    these days a hidden canvas
hangs on a chemical factory wall
           florid
    as a startled moon
    shot through a circle of light

    words are flames again

      there was a thought then
          that fertiliser
     could pay for poetry
pigeon droppings
could redress the balance

    grow white chrysanthemums

who knows if love
    can burn the soul
    rise like a phoenix
when water walls
  are flowing
    like wine

as I watch you soar
  into the sword
swallowed sky
    the flame-throwers
    have left the ring

censored ~~words~~ sing

only the festive hold their calm
      only the festive
    breathe on glass
    apologise
    to the full fat moon

First Impressions Through a Kaleidoscope

Oh, the trench coat, tight-waisted!
I still hear my steely-blue stilettos
Climb back streets, city bones rattling a chorus
Swallows through rafters make a choir
Towers are scaled in peach light
Cats murmur in alleys

Beyond the tulip stands
Coroneted knaves burst their uniforms
Geese get a bad name
Walking the curfew in strides
First impressions have feathered hearts
The bus will take us back to the airport at nine

Sound shell voices before us
Floodlit in the pilgrim night

*

But before this we must extract rabbit ears
From a bear's jaw
Crawl back from a windbreak of pine

Between the dog and the wolf a fox print
And a lynx falling into fractals
Star pooling in a rare pagination

Those books that travelled across war zones
Those graphic shiny glass micro lives
Are a lucent geometry

And as cousins picnic in the wood
Softened by curds and weighing the differences
It all adds up in the trivial and the sublime

You lose a love of algebraic reason
Gain a pound of electromagnetic art

*

We are not Paris said Sirje
We are overlooked in the silent symphony
Of form and meaning
We are fable not fjord nor cubo futurism
Our universal mannequin
Stillness
Deconstructs the folk and lore

We are not the only freelance dance
The language of music and movement
We are the first century Ests
The homeland of Skype
And KaZeA
The most literate and the least religious
Tere Tere Tere

tere – hello

Maps

the cartographers are busy
realigning
the black and red ink
reactor graph
in the margins with a smudge of art rage

>   cities, towns, valleys trespassing their cursives
>   into crosshatched neighbourhoods

port names are swimming out to sea
escaping
the temptation
of green verges
and the kinship of flowing rivers

>   the knives are out in biro
>   soon they will pass into proofs

swept clean of the living who are
somewhere
out of sight in unfamiliar postcodes
where inroads are strident
bright orange lines

>   in school in miniskirts
>   three Baltics, two Poles, a French girl

outsiders
sitting where the air barely ripples
the paper
we're contemplating volcanoes
and the geography of music

Sunset Behind St Olaf's With Chemicals

a stalker shot in the zone, cinematic overkill
where the toxins shoot back
& the renovated ferry terminal practices
industrial chic over steps & bridges

after the propaganda
only the artists inhabit the factory
only the tourists breathe its invisible fumes
shrugging off the tilting beams

wander the makeshift harbour
art exhibits its power plant, slick ferries
wait on sea glass, still as a frozen grave
in the distance lights are blushing

and the space in-between?
only 50 miles to fresh fin air

This poem references the 1987 Estonian film *The Stalker*, partially shot in Tallinn's rundown discarded chemical factory.

Night Poetry

:: and while we sleep

    frost   spectres
    wolf   floods
    spectres of   wolves
    floods of spectres   frozen
    frosty wolves   flooding spectres

always when we sleep the bank doors bolted under frost
always when we sleep ghosts of hounds flooded by moonlight
through blinkless snowy air
footsteps casually
leaving

We could have been harlequins

after Marie Under's 'The Full Moon'

In chequered coats
Moonbeams in our hats
Tumbling in air for Columbine
For all the good we did

We could have been Tõll
White shipped to another land
Mint-green as the strange muzzled dogs
While your moon cracked in golden patches

We could have come earlier
Sounded the sirens, screeched
With gulls over sea foam and land lock

But the sly paw has left your breast now
The incubus has fled the threshold
In breathing streets only snow flutters

Marie Under (1883–1980) was a celebrated Estonian poet. She was a founding member of the Siuru (firebird) literary movement.

The Sea

Oh my sea
You sure have broad hips
And bouncy thighs
– Kalju Lepik

Why not eat its consumables
Map its curves and salty milk
If we are to walk on its thrashing naked skin
Before it turns its back on us

From the rocky point
We are never surprised by the spit and spurt
Or its soft touch
Mooning at our dodgy moorings

We try to dress you in some holy state
But your tongue flicks the grass skirts of sea cows
The scaly wounds of sticklebacks
Washes us in brine

Toss us senseless
    Toss us south
        Toss us a hand
            Breaststroke
                Backstroke
                    Floundering

We leave you teasing the swimmers on your lap
Never serious when you can lick our paddling feet

Kalju Lepik (1920–1999) was a notable Estonian poet.

Baltic Fox

written in a hail
of match and spark
the skies here shine
with ultraviolet intrusion

quick you run slow you run
from dens of impermanence
fox red dreams
evergreen needle nests

how lively your rush of bronze resolve
your triangular face slicing shadows

a quiescent polar wind
blows its flash geometric
in folds with creases
light strobe
            bow shock
across parchment night
while you hunt
in the demigodly spray

there is a clap and curtsey as you run
across the clearings of hungry ghosts

this theatre you own
this landscape
unfolding in pitch angles
with plasmoids

holds you in its dome
floodlit sharp-eyed pert
your ears pricked to a shot
of whistling lead

The glorious white of light

              tight   these jeans
have run their course   indigo &
  pedalling backwards   time triangular days &
             spangled   anglo hills
          rapla farms   their perfumed blooms
        windows glazed   uncracked
           birds migrate   my wings
               unclipped   music hidden
       like sea rolling drunk   in waves
           a cradle a coracle   only worlds
                are spinning   flowers flow
               where flowers   flow oh

www.ingramcontent.com/pod-product-compliance
Lightning Source LLC
Chambersburg PA
CBHW062200100526
44589CB00014B/1883